A Posy of Memories

A Selection of Poems
By Renée D. Smith

Carol
I hope you enjoy my little book of poems.

Renée Smith

A PEACEFUL CORNER

There is no peace,
No quiet.
Do this. Do that.
No, you can't have a cat.

I'll sit on the lavvy, that's what I'll do.
What the rich call a loo.
In the yard, in the dark.
See the stars, hear the rain.
Just imagine you're on that plane.

I can read the paper on the lavvy.
Cut in squares on string so snazzy.
Not like next door, ever so posh.
With real toilet paper and loads of dosh.

When I grow up I'll have a throne
With magazines all around.
For you to read and sit and hum.

Certainly not for wiping your bum.

The Old Tin Bath

It's freezing in the bath tonight
I'm really very cold.
That's because I'm next to last cos I'm not very old.

My Dad goes first cos he's a man.
He pours the water from the pan

The water swishes round and round
And sometimes splashes on the ground.
The fire burns down to a rosy glow.
I'll get a clout if I'm too slow.

The old tin bath is getting rusty.
It hangs in the yard and gets really dusty.
Friday night oh what a job heating the water on the hob.
My mother gets into a right old state.
We've got to be done by half past eight.
So rub and scrub or they'll be late for the pub.

Just once a week across the street, there goes the clatter of their feet.
I lie quiet and very still.
My head pressed close to the window sill.

I hear the band strike up a note.
A song breaks out from someone's throat.

A comforting sound that fills the night
And floods my dreams with a soft glowing light.
Safe and warm in a bell of sound
Until next Friday comes around.

Coal

Fossil gold is a lump of coal.
Rich and black
Tip it out of the sack.

Watch it burn.
It's your turn to pile on the slack.
God it hurts my back shifting this coal down the hole.

Clear out the grate and remove all the slate.

Scrumple the paper and pile on the wood.
It's stacked in the corner in that old tub.

Put the blower into place
Hold up the paper.
No! Not near your face.

Slice the bread not too thin.
Slide the fork carefully in.
Hold it near the rosy glow

Melt the butter ever so slow.

A delicious smell fills the air.
Shadows dance everywhere.
The only way to make your toast
Whilst your little toesies roast.

Don't sit too close or you'll regret it.
Legs like corned beef, you'll never prevent it.

The price of coal that fossil gold
Can't be counted in shillings and pence
At the price of life sadly spent

In the dark! **where's the sense?**

She's Only a Girl

Don't bother with her, she's only a Girl.

Don't educate her she's only a Girl.

She's only fit for wed and bed
Don't put ideas into her head

Teach her to cook and scrub the floor.
Teach her to endure and not ask for more.

Girls should really know their place
Not sit and read and stare into space.
Tell her she's stupid and tell her she's thick.
It works much better than using a stick.

Don't let ideas into her head
Teach her to wash and make the bed.
She's only a girl, not really a pearl.

What a mistake, what a fool
A daughter is a precious jewel.

Blow out the candle and ring the bell.

Break the wicked witch's spell.

A diamond and ruby I now hold
Growing fast as I grow old.

Never to hear the dreaded spell

SHE'S ONLY A GIRL, SO WHAT THE HELL!

The Perfect Mother

See that Lady over there,
She's the Perfect Mother

The one with the Golden Hair.

I would have liked to be like her, so loving and so giving
Patient to the bitter end and oh so very forgiving.
She always knew just what to do for every state occasion.
Never a hair out of place, not even running to the station.

I tried so hard to do it right.
To keep you safe in the dark, dark night.
To protect you from the cold and flu and
Wrap you up against the foggy, foggy dew.

But sometimes I got tired and ratty.
I was hopeless at knitting – it used to get all tatty.

I tried to cook the jam and ham and do all those wonderful meals with spam.

I wanted to help you more at school, but I was the dunce who broke all the rules.

So you'll have to forgive me for failing the test.
It's difficult to be good when you've always been the pest.

But you are the jewels in my crown and I tried so hard not to let you down.

So when you have children of your own, and you are sitting on a difficult throne,

Remember you can only do your best.
You'll make mistakes like all the rest.

So when you see that Lady over there,
The perfect lady with the golden hair,
She's had her trials like all the rest and
I'm sure she felt she didn't do her best.

Wellie Bobs and Knickers

Wellie bobs – What emotions
Pain and shame – Bliss and Dry
Rich and Poor
Which is now at your door?

Wet feet, Cold Feet
Grey Socks, Holey Socks
Always wanting White Socks.

White Knickers, Tight Knickers
Why are mine baggy Knickers?
If only I had loads of Knickers.

Oh what bliss now to have
White Knickers, Pink Knickers
Skimpy Knickers – Loads of Knickers

Rich to me is, I have found,

Lots of children running around

In Dry Feet, White Feet, Straight Feet

Neat Feet

Never Freezing Cold Feet.

The Tomboy

Be in our gang the boys all said
She packs a punch, so mind your head.

She can climb a tree and make a hook
To help us swing across the brook.

Just call her Ren, she can be one of the men.
Have you ever seen her build a den?
She can ride a bike without a brake
She's not really a girl
Don't make that mistake.

But underneath this hard veneer
A little girl was lost in fear.
Wanting to be one of the crowd
Afraid that she would not be allowed.

Then one day they saw through her disguise
The scales fell from their boyish eyes
She's developing breasts
Oh what a pest.

This den's for men not stupid hens
We've been such prats,
Girls can't do that.

Nightmares

Mummy hold my hand there's a monster over there

See I can see his toes peeping out from underneath the stairs

Mummy there's a crocodile underneath my bed
Is he going to chase me and bite off my head?

Mummy can I come in your bed its oooh so safe and warm
I'll snuggle in the bed clothes until it's almost dawn

Can I have a drink of water I am oh so thirsty too

I have a poorly leg and my tummy's hurting bad
I had a nasty dream and I feel so very sad.

Please let me come in your bed

I'll curl up really small, like a little tiny mouse
You won't notice me at all.

Oh look the moon has almost gone – I think it's nearly day.

Is it 8 o'clock yet?
Can I go out to play?

My Dad

When I was a little girl I longed for fairy things.

I walked through bluebell woods and looked for fairy rings

I wanted ruby slippers and a wand to do magic things.

My Dad did his best to make my dreams come true

He showed me a special tree and we knocked upon the wood
We whispered to the fairies that I'd been very good

"Could I have a dog, a little one would do?"

"Dad, do you believe in fairies?"

"Yes I do"

I came home from school one day and there to my surprise
A little black dog with shiny sparkling eyes.

When I was very little we were very poor.

My Dad worked very hard to keep the wolf from the door

So the fairies must have brought my dog
And left it in the basket on
the floor

Cos otherwise it would have been eaten
By that wolf outside the door!!

The Old Old Man

He sits in his chair and dreams and stares.
His golden years but does anyone care?

A frail old man, shuffling and slow.
He was once the head of the show.
Sometimes his brain is as sharp as a tack.
Sometimes his memories come flooding back.

Now and then he is lost and confused.
He can't remember which are his shoes.
Where are the children he loves so dear?
Busy, too busy to lend an ear.
They've heard it all before you know.
God! They think why is he so slow?
But if you take the time to listen
His eyes light up and begin to glisten.
A living history book before you.
How could his story possibly bore you?

So as his life slips away,
Remember! This might be you one day.

Give him your arm and give him a hug.
Help him to steady his shaking mug.

And when his candle is at last snuffed out
Raise a glass of his favourite stout.

Salute the life now complete.
He enriched your life and left it sweet.

The Boss

Do you know Mr Grim Nasty?
He works just down the hall.
He's got dark hair and he's really rather tall.

He comes in every morning and he grunts and groans and frowns,
Until he's had his coffee and then he lifts one brow.
Better get the post open or there'll be an awful row.

"Bring your pad and pencil I have something to import,
A very lengthy letter or some boring monthly report".
"Now get it typed quickly, I haven't got all day!"
I scurry back to my p.c. to get out of his way.

Lunchtime, what a relief he's gone off through the door, to stretch his legs, have a bite and maybe a pint or two or more.

At two o'clock, amazing! A miracle has occurred,
Mr Grim Nasty has disappeared, he is definitely no more.

A smiling kindly man comes sauntering through the door.

"Hello sweetheart, how are you, have you nearly done?"
"I've brought you a rose, some chocolate and a delicious current bun".

"You look nice today or did I forget to say?

I do wish the 'afternoon man' was here everyday.

The clock is ticking now, tomorrow will soon be here.

Mr Grim Nasty, he's not so bad, he's really quite a dear.

In fact I rather like him, his bark's much worse than his bite,
And I'm sure I've heard him giggle,
When he thinks I'm out of sight.

The Dreaded Lump

Oh what's that, is it a lump?
No of course not, no I'm fine
I'll check tomorrow I'm sure there'll be no sign
Just my imagination, forget it, let it be
Go to sleep don't worry and in the light of day
Nothing's ever quite so bad, or so the text books say.

I woke up next morning and the lump was still around.
My heart was thumping fast and my chin upon the ground

The doctor was so very kind; you have a lot upon your mind,
But this is not the end of life, a new beginning after a momentous fight.

We will build a breast it will be as good as new
and if you like graft a nipple on it too.

Your hair has been your Crown in Glory, it will grow again.
You will laugh at all the wigs you wore, the reds the blondes the browns,

The day you were Madonna strutting round the town

The Doctor, he was right you know, the fight was long and hard
Sometimes I felt really thin, sometimes like a lump of lard. Sometimes full of hope, sometimes very low.

Now and then I felt confused not knowing where my life would go.

But here I am fit and well, I fought the fight and won.

I have seen my children grow and my grandchildren too.
So If I can beat that dreaded lump,

YOU CAN TOO!!!

Renée Smith
Diagnosed with Breast Cancer
December 1993

Had a mastectomy and reconstruction.
Still going strong.

The Crooked House Tea Rooms - Windsor

Come in to our Tea Rooms,
Please take a seat.
Our Cakes are Fresh our Scones so sweet.

Specialist Teas loose from the bush.
Dried to perfection
Not to be rushed.

Teacakes, Crumpets, Fine Pastries and Puds
Hot meals and Theme meals
So wholesome and good.

The Crooked House came by its name
From unseasoned timber used for the frame
This gave it a tilt and also its fame.
To miss eating here would be **such** a shame.

A mysterious history, this old Butcher's shop
With a secret passage once used, now blocked.
From Windsor Castle to Old Market Cross
Intriguing, exciting, the meaning now lost.

Kings and commoners have all gathered here
To drink in the warmth and wonderful cheer.

So please come in and take a seat!
Watch the guards!
Have a rest!

Take the weight off your feet!

Birthday Cake

There's a little star in heaven shining down on you

Sent by all the Angels to help you when you're blue.

So on this "Special Day" when you're 21 again
They helped me make a birthday cake with candles all aflame.

Now I know that you like fruit cake and sometimes like it plain.

Dates and walnuts are delicious,

But Guess What?

It's Chocolate Cake Again!!!!

Pat's Birthday

It's such a Special Treat to have a friend like you.

With such a gentle nature who lifts you when you're feeling blue.

And what a cultured voice,
You should be on the stage
Or narrating talking books as you leaf through every page.

So I hope you had a good day

Never mind that you were out when all the boys and girls called
Because I know what they would shout

"Happy Birthday,
With many more to come".

And "oh we are so lucky to have such a lovely
Mum!"

Friendship

Your friends are the jewels in your heavenly crown.

They will be there for you when others let you down.

Don't use them, abuse them: don't treat them with disdain.

One day when you need them, you'll find you've flushed them down the drain.

A caring arm around you is better than any doctor's pill.
It will ease the pain of a broken heart and care for you when you are ill.

So treat them with respect, handle them with care, and show them that you love them.

Remember them in your prayers.

Count them as your blessings, name them one by one.

Think of all their kindness and what they've already done.

But you must do your part and help them heal their hearts, because they'll have troubles too, when they only think of you!

The Passing of a Dear Friend

Dear Charmaine

I rang your number late last night
To hear your voice once again.
To ease the ache inside my heart and take
Away the pain
I won't be sad, but only glad for all the hugs
You gave me.

I'll think of crabbing on Mudeford Quay and
All that lovely herbal tea.
Chilli 'Cry' Carne and Takeaways too
And all the things I learnt from you.

That praise and kindness melt the hardest heart
And you will always be near us even though we are apart.

How to make ice-cream without the
Dreaded ice-cream maker.

I bet you're busy doing it now for the angels and our heavenly maker.

May the Lord Bless you and keep you and hold
You in his arms. Shine his light upon you and keep you safe and warm.

Everyone is missing you, your smiles, your laughs, your frowns
And that

'How you doing Dude'
I miss that lovely sound

Today

Lord help me through this stressful day, to smell the flowers on the way.

Hear the birds and see the trees tossed about by a gentle breeze.

Feel the sun on my frowning brow.

Listen to the gentle crunch of the grazing cow.

Hear the cry of a newborn child and feel the warmth of a loving smile.

And when I go to bed at night, let me sleep in the arms of the Lord Safe and tight.

The Poem

This isn't a poem it doesn't scan
Might as well throw it down the pan.

Go to school you silly fool
A poet needs to learn the rules.

Nothing that comes from the heart
Will ever make a poet start.

I don't agree this from me
A moment of thought cannot be bought.

So open up your narrow mind
And leave your prejudices far behind

The pen is mightier than the sword
So if you're feeling very bored
Leave me to ponder on my past
To cleanse my aura with a blast
To use a crystal deep yet bright
And dispel the terrors of the night.

© Renée D. Smith 2013

All rights reserved. No poem in this collection may be reproduced in whole or in part by any method or in any medium without written permission.

The author has asserted her right to be identified as the author of this work in accordance with the Copyright, Designs and Patents Act 1988.

First published in 2013

Printed in Great Britain
by Amazon.co.uk, Ltd.,
Marston Gate.